MEMOIR WRITING IN 6 EASY STEPS

Your life counts!

MEMOIR WRITING IN 6 EASY STEPS

YOUR LIFE COUNTS!

SUE ROUPP

HenschelHAUS Publishing, Inc.
Milwaukee, Wisconsin

Copyright © 2018 by Sue Roupp

All rights reserved. No part of this publication may be reproduced, distributed or transmitted in any form or by any means, including photocopying, recording, or other electronic or mechanical methods, without the prior written permission of the publisher, except in the case of brief quotations embodied in critical reviews and certain other noncommercial uses permitted by copyright law. For permission requests, please write to the publisher, addressed "Attention: Permissions Coordinator," at the address below.

HenschelHAUS Publishing, Inc.
2625 S. Greeley St. Suite 201
Milwaukee, WI 53207
www.henschelHAUSbooks.com

HenschelHAUS books may be purchased for educational, business, or sales promotional use. For information, please email info@henschelHAUSbooks.com

ISBN: 978159598-560-6
E-ISBN: 978159598-561-3
LCCN: 2017948155

DEDICATIONS

First and foremost, to my husband and children, who are the very foundation of my writing life, always providing solid love and encouragement in generous and kind ways.

To my old friend and mentor, Lorraine Kawalek, who used to leave me voicemail messages, "You'd better finish your book before I die." I didn't make it in time, but she remains in my memory an inspiration.

To my dear friend, photographer Nancy (Schroeder) Gutrich, always cheering me on. To good friend and author of many books, Catherine M. Wallace, PhD, who always has my back. To longtime friend Harriet Claire Wadeson, PhD, said, "Why isn't your book out there?" I was an early editor of her most recent book, "Journaling Cancer in Words and Images: Caught in the Clutches of the Crab."

To Kira Henschel, HenschelHAUS Publishing,
who took a chance on my work being successful.

To every single person I have had the privilege to teach around the country and locally over the years, I say thank you. Your willingness to explore your creativity through your writing always delights, energizes, and amazes me. It is in helping others achieve their writing goals that forms the basis of my teaching. I love what I do—and I love seeing the look of joy on writers' faces when they create something they thought they could not do.

REMEMBER: There is no perfection. There is only good enough.
And good enough can be great!

TABLE OF CONTENTS

Introduction 1

Step 1: Characters / Narrator 7
Step 2: Scenes 25
Step 3: Conflict, and Its Cousin, Anger 37
Step 4: Dialogue 45
Step 5: Theme / Secrets 57
Step 6: Beginning and Ending 63

Wrapping It Up 73
References 77
Acknowledgments 79
About the Author 81

INTRODUCTION

There you sit. Alone. Memories of an event, or from your life, tumble around in your brain. *Where to begin? What to include?* A word-processing document on your computer screen stays blank. You take a deep breath. Pen and paper wait.

Why would anyone besides family members or friends read my memoir? I can't write. Who would care? My memories are like an attic stuffed full of people, scenes, events, conflict, happiness, miserable times, successes, failures and so many images. I can't think.

A voice in your head whispers to you: "Who do you think you are writing a memoir? You will never get it done. You aren't good/smart enough." That voice lives in the high-rent district in your brain. It is your critical lodger. He or she is a deadbeat. A freeloader chiseling out a space in your brain who needs to be evicted. It isn't so easy. It's not like you can press delete and this voice dripping with ridicule can be turned off. The voice stops you every time you try anything that makes you feel vulnerable, or anything that is new.

What to do? You have to learn to co-exist with this negative space occupier. **TIP**. Right now, imagine this voice as a person in your mind. Did you do it? Now put your arms around that person (Does the person look like a parent, or yourself?) and say, "It's ok, I've got this now." Then take a deep breath. Put your fingers on your keyboard or pick up your pen and paper and type or write these words in big, bold letters:

MY LIFE COUNTS

Let me whisper a secret in your ear: people read memoirs to learn both from other people's successes and from your failures.

Readers want to know how you lived your life. How you dealt with a happy or difficult childhood, or with illness, or financial problems, job changes, relationship issues, and the inevitable other things popping up on life's journey. Really. They do.

We live in a worldwide community of human beings, each one struggling to find their way in this world. We humans share, more or less, common feelings of love, anger, dislike, judgment, a need for security, and so much more. We need to tell others how we survived our situations. We need to write about the times, small and large, when we felt both powerless and powerful.

All individuals on the planet are the heroes of their own life dramas. That life comes packaged complete with all the elements we see in novels: conflict, joy, anger, success, failure, sadness, determination...the list goes on.

Introduction

Remember: What you choose to write in your memoir is your view of your life. Not a sibling's view, parental view, spouse's view, family or friend's view of your life (although those views might be included to provide conflict or support). It is ***your*** view of what happened to you or what happened to your parents, or others in your life.

Memoirs come in various types: a particular event in your life, chronicling your parents' or grandparents' lives, writing historical memoirs about a particular time in history, writing about your very own amazing journey through life and more.

What kind of memoir are you considering (circle one or more):

- Your own journey? Yes. No.
- Your parents' journey? Yes. No.
- Your grandparents' journey? Yes. No.
- An event in your life? Yes. No.
- Other?_____

Good for you! You are now on the road to writing your memoir. You thought you couldn't do it. I am here to tell you that **you can write a memoir** and we will do it together, one step at a time.

Memoirs are grouped into two general categories:

1) Writing about your own life, or
2) Writing about an event that happened in your life (surviving a disaster, a medical situation, a war, changing jobs, immigrating to another country...)

Memoir Writing in 6 Easy Steps

Remember that critical roommate in your brain? "You're not a writer," he or she says. "How could you even think of sharing this with someone?"

The system I have developed over years of teaching classes and workshops, giving keynote addresses, hosting a two-year TV show, then working with authors in developmental editing, reduces that voice to a tiny, babbling, barely heard version of itself.

The creative, positive side of your brain is **right now** growing word by word. Remember to be patient with yourself. Have the confidence to know you can sort out the people to include in your book, how to write a scene, build tension, overcome failures, and share your wisdom as you go along.

MEMOIR THEME
(at this moment in time)

As you look back on your life, what would you say was a theme? of your life. Remember, this is not written in stone and

innocence	answers	optimism	faith	loss	family	identity
gunshot	greed	heroism	sacrifice	strength	isolation	aging
solace	vengeance	displacement	separation	technology	injustice	vanity
failure	good/evil	solace	death	perfection	escape	control
racism	temptation	surrender	tradition	health	healing	sorrow
education	love	safety	betrayal	nationalism	power	nature

Introduction

can change as you write your memoir. Here are some theme suggestions:

CHOOSE ONE OF THE THEMES LISTED IN THE TABLE OR ONE OF YOUR OWN.
(Remember—you can always change it!)

WRITE YOUR MEMOIR THEME HERE

_____

YOU are a writer of consequence or you would be doing something else.

*Let's begin our journey in **6** easy steps.*

> There is no such thing as perfection; there is only good enough. We can strive to make something good but perfection is a myth that keeps us from achieving our goals.
> — Sue Roupp

Memoir Writing in 6 Easy Steps

Notes

STEP 1: CHARACTERS / NARRATOR

In writing our memoir we will include people who are or were important to us in one way or another. Some people helped us, some hindered us, some mentored us, some did us physical or verbal damage, some laughed at us or made us angry, some were wise, others gave bad advice, some we trusted and they came through; some we trusted and they betrayed our trust.

We call these people *characters* in our memoir—just as we would call them characters in fiction writing. In memoir writing, characters include family, friends, acquaintances, employers, employees, military officers and enlisted men and women, and countless others. These people are called major and minor characters.

You are the *narrator* in your memoir. What is a narrator? It is the voice, the "I," who tells the story. You narrate the story of your life every day. You tell friends, workers, relatives about what happened during your day. Who did what to whom, how did it turn out, how did you feel about whatever the event was.

Memoir Writing in 6 Easy Steps

Our wants or wishes or needs are a driving force in our lives. As the narrator of your memoir, you look back upon your life. Sometimes you hold back from talking about your wants, wishes, or needs. Sometimes our wishes come true, then we regret our wishes. What is a wish of yours that came true? Or a wish that did not come true?

Maybe we have achieved some of our wants or wishes, but our needs may or may not have been met. Maybe even as children, our needs were or were not met. Why is this important? Because readers will identify with our emotional and physical struggle to get our needs met.

Did things happen that made your life easier—or harder?

Were there people you trusted who disappointed you? People who came through for you? We may have made discoveries. The narrator can write about where, when, how things happened. Did you benefit from your discoveries or not?

We may have lost things, then found them (or not). These things can be tangible (phones, wallets, passports, papers, keys, etc.) or they can be relationships, knowledge (ideas).

In our memoir, we find things out, we solve problems (or not), we find money (or not), opportunities (or not). You, as the narrator, become a storyteller within a memoir.

We look at the ordinary things in our life as well, as the extraordinary (as a child or as an adult). Some things that are ordinary are:

- sleep – waking up and going to sleep
- going to a job – or not

Step 1: Characters / Narrator

- doctor/dentist appointments
- preparing food – or not
- taking classes
- calling someone at particular times
- grocery shopping
- food – comfort food, special occasion dining, holiday food, silly food you crave
- celebration of holidays – or not
- children/grandchildren/spouses/relatives
- communicating with others: email, phone, letters, texts, funny or silly ways to communicate
- meditating or praying
- events (looking forward to some or dreading others)

How do we show we are excited, shy, scared, happy, sad, energetic, depressed, anxious, laid back, and other emotions? Do you (or others) catch their breath, do your hands shake, do you smile a lot? Do you hide your emotions or share them?

MAJOR CHARACTERS. These are the people central to our lives. They keep popping up, whether they are your immediate family, wife, husband, children, extended family, teachers, mentors, friends, doctors who helped (or hindered you) through a difficult life event, or friends. In other words, these are the three to five major characters who keep reappearing in our lives. They may have died, but the memory of them is always with us (whether we want to remember them or not).

MINOR CHARACTERS. Some people wandered into our life or situation to offer good or bad advice, to be there for us, to help or hurt us, to lead us down the wrong road, to laugh at us, to share information, and so on. These people we call *minor characters*. They only appear from time to time during our lives and then disappear. They stimulate or slow down action, offer a joke or laugh to relieve tension, put us down, pick us up, hover over us in our thoughts. There are countless variations.

WRITING ABOUT CHARACTERS. How in the world do we show who our characters are to others? How do we bring them to life (even if they have passed on)? You know too much about them and in memoir writing, you want to choose some details that show the reader their style. Here are several examples.

- In his 1925 novel *Arrowsmith*, Sinclair Lewis used a single sentence: "Mr. Tozer was thin and undistinguished and as sun-worn as his wife, and like her, he peered, he kept silence and fretted."
- "Dr. Swenson is a pretty, blond, young woman in a spacious new office building with blond furniture. Because she looks so young, I ask her how long she has been with North Shore, and she gives me her history—something like eight years, going back to training at Hopkins. It must be a sign of old age that everyone looks young enough to be my grandchild." (*Journaling Cancer in Words and Images/Caught in the*

Step 1: Characters / Narrator

Clutch of the Crab, by Harriet Claire Wadeson, Ph.D, LCSW, ATR-BC, HLM.)

- "Bad, he says to me. They've taken his teeth out, and tears river down the crow's feet of his tough Indian face. Bad. Bad. Bad." (*Lit*, by Mary Karr)

NARRATOR/HERO. Is the person telling the story. In a memoir, it is YOU who are the narrator. Memoirs are therefore written in the first person, using "I," "my," etc. Here is an example from *Forward from Here* by Reeve Lindbergh:

> *There have been one or two horrible times in my life, as there are in too many lives, when the "ongoingness" my mother taught me to value was interrupted in a radical way and neither daily rhythms nor the discipline of writing could restore my balance.*

SORTING OUT PEOPLE IN YOUR LIFE. You may find it hard to sort out the people in your life. Who was significant? Who was not? Could important people be:

- family of origin/current family
- friends
- mentor/therapist/counselor/religious adviser
- employer/teacher/co-worker
- people you met at work
- someone who surprised you with help when you needed it

Memoir Writing in 6 Easy Steps

- as a child someone who taught you something you didn't know
- did you wish someone was a friend or mentor?
- people who served you in some way (medical, other service people)
- people who hindered you
- travel friends or family

Have you ever read a book where you had to make a list of the characters (major and minor) to keep track of them? As writers of a memoir, we need to know our characters and define these characters for ourselves.

We can't include everyone in our memoir but people recurring during our lives and many we came in contact with along the way will be key to the ongoing stories in our life or event memoir. As the narrator, you might want to include:

- what haunts you
- did you forgive anyone
- dwellings that mean something to you

FLASHBACKS/NARRATIVE ARC. Readers will want to know how things are going in your current life. Inevitably, you will flash back to an earlier time in your life. You, as the narrator, have to think about how you have changed from wherever your memoir began until the present. This is called a *narrative arc*.

Step 1: Characters / Narrator

Or you can begin in the middle of something memorable (good or bad) that happened to you, then *flash forward* to your current life, reflecting on how that memorable event changed your life. Either way, you are developing a narrative arc of your life.

The narrative arc can go one of two ways:

1. You begin at the beginning of your life (I discourage this because your memoir slows down as if on a conveyor belt timeline and the reader may lose interest);

2. You begin in the middle of a powerful scene (it can be something large – getting a dream job or winning a prize or getting married or…it can be something terrible that happened as in abuse, abandonment, divorce, physical harm etc.). By beginning in the *middle of the action,* your reader will be hooked to find out what happened and will continue to read on in your memoir.

Theme. As described previously, you may have written a word that describes your life and find that the scenes you remember seem to fit into that theme.

THE OTHER. Your memoir is about your own personal life, but it is also about what I call the *other*—places, people, and things that are important to you. Things or places that you treasure—or don't like or use anymore.

Memoir Writing in 6 Easy Steps

- FOOD YOU LIKE OR CAN'T EAT ANYMORE
  _____

- FAVORITE/LEAST FAVORITE TOWN IN THE WORLD
  _____

- FAVORITE/LEAST FAVORITE PIECE OF CLOTHING
  _____

- TOOLS YOU LOVE OR DON'T USE ANYMORE
  _____

- CARS THAT CAUSED YOU TROUBLE
  _____

- YOUR FAVORITE MAJOR PERSON IN YOUR LIFE RIGHT NOW
  _____

- PLACES WHERE YOU LIKE TO EAT
  _____

- PLACES WHERE YOU HATE TO EAT
  _____

- WHAT DID YOUR FATHER/CARETAKER LIKE TO EAT/DRINK
  _____

- WHAT DID YOUR MOTHER/CARETAKER LIKE TO EAT/DRINK
  _____

- WHAT DO YOU LIKE TO COOK
  _____

- NAME SOMEONE VERY DIFFERENT THAN YOU ARE
  _____

- THE WEATHER YOU HATE
  _____

- THE WEATHER YOU LOVE
  _____

Step 1: Characters / Narrator

- WHERE DID YOU GROW UP?
  _____

- PLACES YOU HAVE LIVED
  _____

- DID YOU LIVE IN A HOUSE, APARTMENT, TRAILER, TENT, HOTEL, BOARDING SCHOOL
  _____

- WHERE WAS YOUR FAVORITE PLACE TO LIVE?
  _____

- WHERE WAS YOUR LEAST FAVORITE PLACE TO LIVE?
  _____

- WHY?
  _____

- BEST ADVICE YOU HAVE RECEIVED
  _____

- WORST ADVICE YOU HAVE RECEIVED
  _____

- ADVICE YOU REJECTED BUT IT TURNED OUT TO BE GOOD ADVICE
  _____

- SOMETHING DUMB THAT STANDS OUT
  _____

- SOME JOB YOU LOVED/HATED
  _____

- A SPECIAL PLACE YOU KEPT SECRET
  _____

- SOME OBJECTS SPECIAL TO YOU
  _____

Memoir Writing in 6 Easy Steps

CHARACTERS
HERE IS THE FUN PART. . .

Write down the **MAJOR CHARACTERS** in your life in the first box. They might be friends, relatives, allies, mentors, religious figures, teachers, coaches, business colleagues, travel partners, life partners, etc.

NO THINKING HERE!

Now write their relationship to you . . .

DO THIS VERY FAST! IT CAN ALWAYS BE CHANGED.

Good for you! You have written down the characters who came to you. Some of them said, "*Me* first!" Others said, "No, *me!*" These are the important people in your life. Aren't you amazed at how many people flood into your mind? Choose four names from this list. Do not put any effort into choosing these names.

Step 1: Characters / Narrator

MAJOR CHARACTER TABLE

Character Name	Relationship	Two details about this person
1.		
2.		
3.		
4.		
5.		
6.		
7.		
8.		
9.		
10.		

Memoir Writing in 6 Easy Steps

Who you choose is not written in stone. These names may change in five minutes or in an hour or tomorrow. For our purposes here, we need **four characters from your list**.

Write in the names of four people you choose into this chart. Here is an example of what that chart might look like:

MAJOR Characters	How Related?
1. John D.	Mentor who died
2. Meredith S.	Sister who fought me over inheritance
3. Tonata W.	Co-worker who lied about me.\
4. Gabriel G.	Friend who helped me out of a tight spot

You can always change who you add or subtract from your list. Now write your own major character names and how they are related in the table.

NAME YOUR MAJOR CHARACTERS	HOW RELATED?
1.	
2.	
3.	
4.	

Step 1: Characters / Narrator

GOOD FOR YOU! You did it? Now you have some of the main characters who will appear and reappear in your memoir. You can rearrange the later when you discover someone else who was more important

WHY ARE WE DEFINING OUR MAJOR CHARACTERS NOW? Because we need to reduce the number of characters in our memoir to just a few.

5 MINUTE WRITING PROMPT

Write very fast (***no thinking***). Four of your characters are at a party. Begin writing with, "Did you know…?"

* * * * *

We also need to make it easier for our readers to see who else was important to us. Readers cannot keep track of more than a few major characters at a time.

MINOR CHARACTERS These people are fascinating. They can deliver information, mentor, hinder, hurt, help, laugh, love us, dislike us, and more. There can be:

- a mischievous friend who doesn't believe you when you share some news;
- a FRIEND who never/sometimes listens to you;
- someone who lies;
- someone who loves you but disappears emotionally or physically;

Memoir Writing in 6 Easy Steps

- someone who tells a secret revealing information;
- someone who fires you; wants to control you, solves your problem and much more...

Our lives are full of these minor characters. They may have played a pivotal role in our lives at one time, either positively or negatively. At the time, you may have thought, "How will I get through this?" Someone appears to help or hinder you. Then that person becomes nothing but a memory.

Minor characters can help with unmet expectations or in winning life's lottery; that is, having everything going your way (although life being life, that doesn't happen).

In any life, from birth to death, we meet all kinds of people. Initially, the members of our family of origin, whatever that may be, are our major character(s). They may remain major characters throughout our life.

As we grow older, our world becomes populated with others: extended family, friends, coworkers, significant others, children, police, firefighters, musicians, artists, the medical community, teachers, counselors—these people who appear then disappear and may or may not reappear later in our lives.

Remember the person who gave you your first job? Your first teacher? The first time you traveled alone? Your first pet? Your first report card? The first time you did something you didn't want anyone to know about? The first time you kissed someone? The first time you held a child's hand? The first time you fell in love? The first time you stood up to someone? The

Step 1: Characters / Narrator

first time you said the word "no" or "yes" to a significant other? The first time you quit a job or a relationship? The first time you were fired, left school, wrote a letter, went to the doctor, had surgery, cried in public?

MINOR CHARACTERS

You are so experienced—now fill in the table below with some minor characters.

WOW! YOU'RE DOING A WONDERFUL JOB!

Character Name	Relationship	Two details about this person
1.		
2.		
3.		
4.		
5.		
6.		
7.		
8.		
9.		
10.		

Memoir Writing in 6 Easy Steps

5 Minute Writing Prompt

Choose four characters from this table. You are at the grocery store one day. All four of your characters are there, but they only know you. They gather around you and you introduce them to one another. Then you ask each of them, "Do you still have…?"

* * * * *

Let's Go Over What You've Learned:

1. **MAJOR CHARACTERS**: These are people who played a major role in your life or, in the case of an event memoir, helped or hindered you in achieving your goal. When you think about your life or event these people immediately come to mind.

    We can't include everyone we have met in our memoir, but we can include those who reappear in our lives, or event, as significant characters.

2. **MINOR CHARACTERS**: These people pop in and out of your life to offer to help, stop you, provide negative or positive information, tell secrets, compete, hurt you, lift your spirits, mentor you, leave you…they come into our lives in infinite variations.

    We only keep them in our memoir if they contribute something to our lives (either positively or negatively).

Step 1: Characters / Narrator

3. **NARRATOR/STORYTELLER:** YOU are the narrator and storyteller of your memoir. No one can tell your story like you can tell your story. Relatives and/or friends may say, "That's not how it happened." You can tell them, "This is MY memoir from my point of view. If you want to write a memoir from your point of view, please do."

NOTE: Memoirs should never be about getting even, or a diatribe against another person. No one reads them. Nor will agents be willing to pitch such stories to publishers. They simply aren't interesting.

If something terrible happened to you, tell the story as you remember it—the reader will see the scene as you experienced it, FROM YOUR POINT OF VIEW, without saying So-and-So is a _____ (fill in the blank).

Memoir Writing in 6 Easy Steps

Notes

STEP 2: SCENES

We think back on our lives and the events we remember in "SCENES."

In our minds are stored endless memories: the first time we didn't feel safe, our first job, where we grew up, moving around the country and how hard it was to make friends, either as a kid or as an adult, our parents' struggles, our siblings' ups and downs, losses, successes, loneliness, job, children, travels, promotions, firings, and of course, many more types of scenes.

How do we get any order out of this jumble of memories, so we can tackle writing our memoir? It isn't as hard as you might think.

You've already corralled major and minor characters. You know you are the narrator (storyteller), and now we have to use those characters to tell our story in scenes.

There are small scenes that often tell your true voice, and there are high-impact scenes that stay with you—and your readers.

Memoir Writing in 6 Easy Steps

Do you want to know more? Great! That means you want to turn the page of a book. Relationships can be close, distant, or in between.

Here is an example of writing a short scene:

| Intro of character season, room, house |

She came into the room with careful steps. The cracked wood floor was dusty and worn. Sarah had no shoes on that hot, late August day. Avoiding splinters from the bare wood, she walked over to the window she had always loved.

The living room window was the same window she saw in her childhood. It had an old storm window still on it. The one with a little crack in the upper left corner. The room was warm, but it didn't matter.

Her tall older brother walked into the room carrying the letter. "Why are you walking around in bare feet?" he asked.

| Second character Object (letter) carries info |

"Force of habit, I guess," Sarah said as she turned toward him. Jimmy stood there in his orange polo and old jeans. He held out his hand. The envelope had been ripped open, its jagged flap upright like a well-worn sail on a boat out in the water too long.

"What's that?"

"Read it, Sarah. It's from the lawyer. Mom's lawyer. Christ, just read it."

| Tension mounts |

Sarah reached for the envelope, then tugged the letter out. "Did you read it already? Wait. It's addressed to me. You opened my letter?"

Jimmy said nothing. He just walked away through the dining room, then the workroom, and out the back door, slamming each door as he went.

Step 2: Scenes

Sarah opened the handwritten letter from Mom's old friend, a lawyer she had known most of her life.

Dear Sarah,

Just wanted to let you know your mom left everything to you. Come into the office ASAP so we can talk about what to do with it all.

Ken Samuels

> Apex of tension
> Scene ends

Mom left all of it to me, Sarah thought. All of what?

"Jimmy, Jimmy!" Sarah yelled, running toward the dining room door to the workshop. "Damn," she cried out, hopping and looking for the splinter in her foot. "Damn!"

What is important in the above scene? Or in scenes you want to include in your memoir?

DETAILS bring the scene to life, adding texture and information for the reader to any scene. The reader sees what you see.

- What does the place look like? Describe the walls, floors, furniture. Is it modern? Old-fashioned? Is there carpeting?
- Is there a TV, cell phone, corded phone?
- Are there trees or landscaping?
- Are there toys, books?
- Is there an automobile? What does it look like? Is it old, new, rusty, well-kept?
- What does the landscape look like? Flat, hilly, dry, green?
- Are there dead flowers, neat beds of flowers, or is the outside unkempt?

- Are there barns, apartment buildings, houses?
- Are the roads hilly, flat, gravel, paved?
- Is there a lake, pond, gravel pit nearby?

BEGINNING, MIDDLE, AND END OF SCENE

We tell stories every day to each other. They have a beginning, middle, and often, but not always, an ending. "Did you hear …?" "Guess what …" "I remember …" are the beginnings of our oral storytelling.

In memoir writing, we reveal our memories through the scenes we remember—maybe an accident we had, or a family member or friend being ill, at time we failed, a time we succeeded, a time we fell in love, a time we were divorced, a time our job changed (for better or worse), and much more.

The **beginning of a scene** can begin anywhere. As I mentioned above, I recommend that it begin in the middle of the action. Characters enter the scene, they see objects, another person(s), or are on the phone, computer, texting, in an office, a room, outside in a boat, around a campfire, in a house, etc.

The **middle of a scene** is where things are discussed (or not) and the story intensifies. Characters can give or take in information, share details, confront tension (or not), revelation may occur, conflict can happen, tension can build.

At the **end of a scene**, characters can leave. If in the beginning or middle of a memoir, the tension can remain. If it is toward the end of a memoir, tension can resolve (or not).

The scene ending does three things:

Step 2: Scenes

1. It may or may not resolve an issue
2. It informs your reader about something important to you
3. It keeps your readers' attention and leads them on to the next chapter.

DIALOGUE

In memoir writing, dialogue is never remembered word for word, but you do remember the important parts of something someone said. If you do not recall a conversation word for word (and who does, unless it's recorded?), don't use quotation marks around the dialogue.

TRANSITION

After writing a scene, there needs to be a transition to a new scene or chapter. Maybe it is a reaction to a situation or a problem. Maybe the problem or what was discussed is talked about. Maybe decisions are made.

CHARACTERS IN SCENES

What do they …

- Wear?
- Smoke (or not)?
- Drink?
- Eat?
- Do their eyes light up when seeing someone, or do they harden?

- How do they stand or sit or walk?
- Do they have health issues?
- Do their faces get red with anger, embarrassment, being noticed?
- Do they like music? What kind?
- Are they withdrawn? Uncaring?
- Are their shoulders hunched? Do they stand erect?
- Is their speech abrupt or do they tell long stories?

IMPORTANT SCENES IN OUR LIVES.

We humans live through scenes in our life every day. Our lives are like random, unscripted movies. Things happen, and often not in sequence. In **MEMOIR SCENES**, we cannot include—nor do we remember—or want to remember—every scene or event. Certain scenes stand out for us and we remember them in **CATEGORIES OF SCENES**.

SCENE CATEGORIES

We tend to group our scenes into:
- Growing up
- Relationships
- Jobs
- Marriage or divorce
- Children
- Successes

Step 2: Scenes

- Failures
- Turning points
- Losses
- Travel
- War
- Medical issues
- _____
- _____
- _____

Fill in the blanks as you think about your life.

SCENES BEGIN, GROW A MIDDLE, AND THEN END

We introduce a scene in the middle of the action.

Do not have a long explanation for a scene. Use an *active voice*, not a *passive voice*. You can explain why the scene is important through the dialogue between the characters or a brief narration.

The construction of a scene goes like this:

- Introduction of the characters
- Problem or resolution of a problem presented
- An issue is resolved or not, but the tension rises
- The end of the scene is like a dissolving camera shot, leading the reader into the next part of your memoir.

Memoir Writing in 6 Easy Steps

Now that you know the construction of a scene, you are probably wondering, "How do I decide which scenes to put into my memoir?"

The scenes in your life, either for a personal or an event memoir, come to the surface of your consciousness as you remember what happened to you in pivotal situations. We remember:

- Happy or sad times
- Challenges / losses / wins
- Laments / changes
- Winning against the odds
- Cooking / eating together or alone
- Traveling to faraway places (the next town or across the world)
- Sports (learning / winning / losing)
- Violence
- Weather
- Love / marriage / divorce / death

Step 2: Scenes

SCENES FOR MY MEMOIR

Name of scene?	Who is in the scene?	Where does it take place?
1.		
2.		
3.		
4.		
5.		
6.		
7.		

5 MINUTE WRITING PROMPT

Take two characters from one scene listed above and have them meet each other. Then have one of them drop something, breaking it. Keep going with the dialogue back and forth. Remember to write as fast as you can. No thinking here! Just see what happens.

Memoir Writing in 6 Easy Steps

HOW TO ORGANIZE THE SCENES AS THEY COME TO YOU

Make a list or chart or spreadsheet as you think of incidents (scenes) that flood your mind: going to school for the first time, falling in love for the first time, an argument, the first time you discovered someone was lying to you, the meals you like (or hate) to cook, the first drink you took, the first time you drove a car or got stopped by the police ...

MORE IMPORTANT SCENES

Name of scene?	Who's in the scene?	Where does it take place?
1.		
2.		
3.		
4.		
5.		
6.		
7.		
8.		
9.		

Step 2: Scenes

Name of scene?	Who's in the scene?	Where does it take place?
10.		
11.		
12.		
13.		
14.		
15.		
16.		
17.		
18.		
19.		
20.		
21.		
22.		
23.		
24.		
25.		

Memoir Writing in 6 Easy Steps

Notes

STEP 3: CONFLICT AND ITS COUSIN, ANGER

You've never had any kind of conflict in your life, right? No parent/child, child/parent, "I want ... you can't have ..." sort of dialogue? How about when a professional person (doctor, lawyer, therapist, religious person, etc.) has said, "This is what I want you to do now ..." and you say, "Do what? Why? I'm not going to do that!"

Let me remind you at this point of something very important: As you write your memoir, you will relive these experiences. You must hold your own heart tenderly, with patience, kindness, and understanding.

Maybe a spouse/partner has said, "You did this to me, and I am really angry." You say, "No, I didn't. How can you say such a thing?" The other person says, "Shame on you for saying that to me ..." or "Shut your mouth!" or "You're so stupid ..." or "You're so ugly ..." or some other awful thing. Or someone dismisses you, waving you away, ending a phone call, not returning your calls, not answering your emails, etc., after you say something you want them to hear.

Or ... You say nothing, then later maybe boil over, finding yourself doing one of two things: yelling or getting depressed. Either way, you feel furious.

Maybe you have been the recipient of verbal or physical abuse—from your family of origin, in your workplace, from your partner, or from other sources. Can you write about these awful times—times when you felt vulnerable, scared, hurt, or humiliated?

I would like to suggest that you include these times in your memoir. Telling your story with an "I" message—as in "I saw this" or "This happened to me" seems the way to go. What you can't do, though, is call others names, or often, use their proper names.

A memoir is not a time to get even with others, but rather a time to tell your own life story, or the story of an event or events that happened over time. Yes, terrible things might have happened and you can describe them and write about them from your point of view (POV).

Some writers change the names of the character(s) who abused or hurt them verbally of physically. Some change location. Many have written about their own abuse or watching others abuse others—from their own POV.

Maybe you are—or have been—in the military and want to write about that time in your life. How do you write about the intense anguish, fear, focus, or killing that went on? I spoke with

Step 3: Conflict and its Cousin, Anger

a man in a rural town who has been an alcoholic since his time in Vietnam. "How do I talk about that?" he said.

I told him, "One word at a time."

He waved me off as he headed to his favorite tavern—for community and to tamp down his memories.

Why is conflict an important sort of thing to include in writing your memoir, even though you may hate to include some of those moments?

CONFLICT IS IMPORTANT BECAUSE IT IS POWERFUL AND IT CARRIES A NARRATIVE ARC THAT HOLDS THE SCENES TOGETHER IN A SINGLE, COHERENT STORY. It can also be informative, a turning point, add tension, get our readers to wonder what will happen so they turn the page. It also allows our readers to feel empathy for you, the narrator of your memoir.

If your readers can see you in times of conflict, they know you know how they feel sometimes. Everyone feels angry and conflicted at certain times and in certain situations. It doesn't matter how these situations turn out; that is, how we react to anger. What matters is this: conflict deepens any character if high emotional situations arise from time to time.

One cannot escape anger, conflict, and struggles in life. I think it comes written into our DNA. As infants, we wail because we are hungry or tired or want something. When those needs are not fulfilled, we feel upset.

Sometimes we cry as adults, but most often, we raise our voices and as an argument goes on, we get louder, right?

Sometimes we back away, we turn inward, then worry afterwards about not standing up for ourselves, or at least saying something—anything. We go over and over those times in our minds, rewriting what happened.

In fact, I often tell writers who are stuck in expressing a high-tension scene, to write the scene the way they wanted it to come out. Of course, you don't include that part in your memoir, but it makes you feel powerful to write the scene using whatever words you want to include in that scene from hindsight. It also allows you to let go of the guilt/shame/delight you may feel in that emotionally charged moment.

DEATH AND REBIRTH SCENES

Often in our lives there comes a time when our assumptions about life change. This may occur while we are searching for something.

Maybe it is getting a college degree with zero finances. Maybe it is traveling somewhere to help others, or maybe it is where the boundaries of who you are become stretched so far the basic notion of who you are has changed.

Maybe you accepted more responsibility than you thought you could handle, but you did it. This is a time-tested, often riveting part of a memoir.

Maybe you stood up to a parent, or a boss, and you never thought you could do it. At that moment, you leave the comfortable notion of who you are and become the hero of your story told through a "death" and rebirth scene. Your heroism can be

Step 3: Conflict and its Cousin, Anger

simply within yourself, or it can be in your job, community, family, with relatives or friends.

Maybe you wanted to get in touch with your creative side, become more assertive. Maybe you felt overwhelmed. Writing about your hidden qualities and the shadows in your life allows others to see your intuitive side.

Yes. You faced your biggest fear. You changed and there you are in a new, undefined role, but your reader is riveted by your actions. Remember, your reader roots for you, identifies with your struggles, and feels less alone knowing someone else in the world has had to struggle at times.

NEGATIVE SCENES

Maybe you were attracted to someone who wasn't good for you. You became involved with someone who turned out to be nasty. It might be that someone who stole from you. Stealing can be a fact: stealing money, goods, or other objects or digital resources. Or it can be someone stealing your pride, rejecting you, mothers or fathers who put you down, military experiences that sear your soul.

CRISIS SCENES

Crises happen to everyone on the planet. Maybe someone you fell in love with showed another side and you felt betrayed and lonely.

If you grew up in an abusive family, or a detached, uninvolved family where you felt neglected, have an intimate partnership with someone who turned out to be abusive, know this: abuse knows no boundaries—not only in the U.S. but around the world.

Emotional and physical abuse exist in the real world. People growing up in homes that were abusive may or may not partner with someone who is abusive. This is a familiar pattern, and without help, can replicate itself.

Think of some times when you were in an argument with someone—it doesn't matter when it happened or who was there.

When you write about these experiences, two things happen:

1. You gain power and control over these memories even though they are difficult to relive; and
2. You just might help someone who reads your memoir about these experiences and help relieve the crushing loneliness they feel when abuse happens to them.

Here are some other times conflict arises:

- A PARTNER/FRIEND/FAMILY MEMBER NEEDS OR WANTS SOMETHING but can't get it without your cooperation—but you don't want to do it;
- A JOB SITUATION arises but there are problems to be resolved;
- YOU HELP A STRANGER and your help makes all the difference in the person's life, even though you did not want to get involved;
- SOMEONE IN A STORE IS RUDE OR NASTY but you do something out of character to stop the situation,

Step 3: Conflict and its Cousin, Anger

stand up for someone else or maybe resolve the situation;

- YOU ARE IN TRAFFIC and get stopped for something you did not do;
- SOMEONE STEALS something from you, and you confront that individual in person, by text, email, snail mail—or not;
- YOU HEAR A SECRET, and now you have to decide what to do about it;
- You're in the MILITARY and you find yourself in a situation you never even thought about;
- or anything else you can think of...

Conflict (who or what?)	Conflict over what issue?

5 Minute Writing Prompt

Write for five minutes about a time you were in a conflict situation and you felt powerless. Then write for five minutes writing about how you would have liked that situation to turn out so you would have felt powerful. *Write very fast. No thinking here.*

Memoir Writing in 6 Easy Steps

STEP 4: DIALOGUE

"*Why should I include dialogue?*"
"*It makes the people you include in your memoir come alive.*"
"*What if I don't remember the conversation exactly?*"
"*No one remembers a conversation exactly unless you are recording the conversation.*"
"*What do I do?*"
"*You remember the gist of a conversation—if it was a discussion or argument about a particular thing. You may not remember every word but you will remember how you felt during this conversation.*"

The trick is this: we carry on in dialogue all day long every day. We report he said/she said to our friends, our family, our co-workers. We don't remember every word of anything—but we do remember what the conversation was about.

Today, or yesterday, or last week—bring into your mind a conversation you had, even if it was just for a few minutes. Did you remember a conversation? Good.

Memoir Writing in 6 Easy Steps

Now write that conversation down—as in (s)he said. (name of person) said.

DO NOT USE ANY ADVERBS IN WRITING DIALOGUE. No *sadly*, or *heatedly*, or *fiercely*. Let the dialogue carry the emotion. The preceding sentence or the sentence after the dialogue might have a person do something that emphasizes the feeling he or she is having.

> From Stephen King, in *On Writing*:
> *"I insist that you use the adverb in dialogue attribution only in the rarest and most special of occasions ... and not even then, if you can avoid it."*
>
> Just to make sure we all know what we're talking about, examine these three sentences:
>
> > "Put it down!" she shouted.
> > "Give it back," he pleaded, "it's mine."
> > "Don't be such a fool, Jekyll," Utterson said.
>
> In these sentences, *shouted*, *pleaded*, and *said* are verbs of dialogue attribution. Now look at these dubious revisions:
>
> > "Put it down!" she shouted menacingly.
> > "Give it back," he pleaded abjectly, "it's mine."
> > "Don't be such a fool, Jekyll," Utterson said contemptuously.
>
> The three latter sentences are all weaker than the three former ones, and most readers will see why immediately. Some writers try to evade the no-adverb rule by shooting the attribution verb full of steroids. The result is familiar to any reader of pulp fiction or paperback originals:

Step 4: Dialogue

> "Put the gun down, Utterson!" Jekyll grated.
> "Never stop kissing me!" Shayna gasped.
> "You damned tease!" Bill jerked out.
>
> The best form of dialogue attribution is *said*, as in *he said, she said, Bill said, Monica said."*

If it is an indirect quotation and not a dialogue you remember word for word, DO NOT USE QUOTATION MARKS IN YOUR MEMOIR. I use it here because this is an excerpt from Mary Karr's book *Lit*.

> "And so it hits me: I have to kiss alcohol goodbye – no half measures, no quibbling, no champagne at the wedding, no valium at the dentist, no codeine for the cough.
> "Ninety meetings in ninety days," she says.
> I don't complain but must've pulled a face.
> "It's like you have cancer," she says, and "coming here is really chemo. It's not a luxury. It's not a help. It's what stands between you and going insane or winding up in the boneyard."

LET'S PRACTICE WRITING SOME DIALOGUE

First of all, dialogue must sound real—just as the person who is talking would say it. If Grandma swears, Include it. If a kid swears, Include it. Think of a conversation—any conversation you had in the past—or even today. It can be about anything. Maybe related to a job, a partner, health, a holiday, food, kids, family, superiors, money, transportation, pets, loss, education, something you found, or something else.

Memoir Writing in 6 Easy Steps

I said: _____

He/she said: _____

I said: _____

He/she said: _____

The words you use cannot be passive. Emotion is embedded in the dialogue you use. What is one person trying to tell the other person? Why? Remember—your reader must identify with you and whatever situation you are describing.

Take your four lines (or so) of dialogue and now add a phrase or sentence after each bit of dialogue describing how it feels.

What if your four words were: *breathe, try, tears, worry*? Here is an example from the book *Paula*, by Isabelle Allende, an event memoir about Ms. Allende's daughter falling into a coma and being very ill. The emotional description is in italics.

> "Here, you have blood on your lips," he said.
> "This afternoon we'll try again, and then tomorrow, and so on, a little more each day, until she can breathe on her own," I resolved, *when I could speak.*
> "Paula may not be able to breathe on her own…"
> "She will, Doctor. I'm going to take her out of this place and it will be easier if she helps me."
> "I suppose mothers know better than anyone else. We will gradually lower the pressure of the respirator

Step 4: Dialogue

to force her to use those muscles. Don't worry, we'll see she gets plenty of oxygen," he smiled, giving me an affectionate pat on the shoulder.

My eyes were blurred with tears as I left the room and rejoined my mother."

Add your dialogue and sentences / phrases here:

Memoir Writing in 6 Easy Steps

Are you getting the hang of it? Yes? No? Sort of? If you struggle with dialogue—and we all do at some point—do this: Speak the dialogue out loud, responses as well. Remember, when we speak to someone, we usually speak in bits or phrases of sentences, rather than in full sentences.

Speaking the dialogue aloud with emotion as if speaking to another person works. Yes, you might feel silly or nuts. In saying dialogue out loud, we sharpen what we remember and what we, or the people in our lives, want to say.

Early on in my writing career at the University of Chicago, I worked with a wonderful, but very tough, teacher. In her writing workshops and in response to a writing prompt, she would make us write for what seemed like an eternity.

Then we had to turn over our pads of paper (longhand writing was preferred—not on a computer) and tell our story out loud. The function of this exercise was to see how we streamlined our story in the oral telling of it.

When we tell a story to another person (even if we are just working out the story within ourselves), we tell the salient facts. When we write a story, we have to include some sort of emotional response. If we are talking with another person we—and the other person—are reading the color in our face, how we stand, turn our head, what feeling (or none) is in another's eyes and so on.

Step 4: Dialogue

If I write this dialogue:

Cary said to me you can't go on this trip.

(*Indirect; remembered dialogue has no quotes*).

I said but I can do it. I know I can.

Do you see how little emotion is in that exchange? The conversation is flat, two-dimensional, and we only get a bit of emotion.

How about this?

Cary said to me you can't go on this trip.
I said, but I can do it. I know I can.
I walked over to my computer desk where I had a few sheets of paper stacked up. Noticing my hand trembled, I picked up the paper. I need to go on this trip, Cary. The paper shook a little as I handed it to her. Here are the figures to show I can do it.

I expanded the dialogue: Hands tremble. Paper shakes. I have the math to prove it is doable. (Why do I have to prove this to Cary?). Your reader now wants to know more.

Occasional dialogue engages the reader. Its function is to convey information and emotional content, it can be funny, and brings energy to your story. It keeps the reader turning the page to see what will happen next.

Memoir Writing in 6 Easy Steps

Screenplays and stage plays are, of course, all written in dialogue. The actors/director interpret the screenwriter's words to make those words come to life.

In memoir writing, our readers interpret our feelings. We engage the reader who can identify with our feelings. We need to have the people we write about have conversations about situations that develop between them—or between others who are in our memoir. It allows the reader to root for you, the hero of your own story.

* * * * *

EXAMPLE OF ADDING DIALOGUE, USING MY OWN MEMOIR AS AN EXAMPLE

I remember when my dad was very ill with a variety of serious illnesses. He was never very communicative as I grew up but worked long hours as a printer for the *Chicago Tribune.* His shifts varied and getting out the editions was time-consuming and pressure filled.

As an only child, I didn't know him well except for his love of opera and art. He had quite a temper (as did my mom) and didn't understand my need to get an education.

In his own way, he would say "Get a job. What good will an education do you?"

Step 4: Dialogue

I moved out at age 18 and worked many jobs to get an undergraduate degree and then went on educationally—my parents came to my degree ceremony, but left before I received my degree. My focus on getting an education created quite a rift between my family and myself. I was "putting on airs," my mom and dad would say.

In his 60s, Dad's various diseases were out of control. Now he was in a hospital and on an experimental medicine. For some reason, my mom didn't want me to spend much time alone with him. Maybe she just wanted to savor every minute of their long marriage. But during one hospital visiting day, she left me alone for a while with him.

A short man with dark hair tinged with gray, he lay on his hospital bed with his head and back tilted more or less upright. I sat next to him in an old cracked leather chair.

All of a sudden, he looked up at the ceiling and smiled a broad smile. Unassisted, he sat up further in bed, reaching out his hands to whatever or whoever he was looking at in that hospital ceiling. His one hand took an imaginary cup with a saucer. His hand pretended to pick up this imaginary cup and put it to his lips, all the while beaming and looking up at the ceiling.

One of his diseases, Parkinson's, caused his body and very soul to shake and had taken his speech away. During these episodes of reaching for a cup of something (repeated verbatim throughout the days), he did not shake at all. His hands were steady. Finally, he lay back down on his pillow.

I said, leaning over to kiss him on the forehead, "I love you." Then I turned around to leave. I looked back at him. Startled, I watched him with no effort sit up in bed, turning his body toward me.

He smiled and in his loud, firm voice said, "I love you." Then he lay back down on his pillow. I said "I love you, too."

My mom was standing in the doorway to the room. "Let's go," she said. It was the last time I saw him. He died soon after that. I wonder if that was Mom's metaphor for his demise soon approaching.

* * * * *

The power of that scene has stayed with me for a lifetime. Do you remember a time when something amazing happened? Something you did not expect, either positive or negative—it doesn't matter.

What matters is how some of your scenes should include some dialogue. I know you remember times where you said something you remember. Include those dialogues in your memoir and others will remember it, too.

Of course, we do remember actual dialogue. There are important (and often interesting scenes) we remember. This is

Step 4: Dialogue

called *direct dialogue*. These conversations are in quotation marks.

On the other hand, *indirect dialogue* is a summary of a conversation and appears in the storytelling narrative. It happens when the reader needs to know the conversation took place, but doesn't need to know the actual words spoken. Indirect dialogue is also used to condense a long conversation.

Then there is dialogue that is *paraphrased*. We remember the gist of a conversation, but not word for word. There are no quotation marks around paraphrased dialogue.

Memoir Writing in 6 Easy Steps

Notes

STEP 5: THEME / SECRETS

You have been writing and thinking about your memoir and maybe what you would choose as the theme of your life changed. At this moment, what would you say the theme of your life during your event or your whole life is? Often, as we sift through our event or personal memoir writing about people we knew and events we are writing about, we see a different theme develop during our lives.

LIFE THEMES

innocence	answers	optimism	faith	loss	family	identity
gunshot	greed	heroism	sacrifice	strength	isolation	aging
solace	vengeance	displacement	separation	technology	injustice	vanity
failure	good/evil	solace	death	perfection	escape	control
racism	temptation	surrender	tradition	health	healing	sorrow
education	love	safety	betrayal	nationalism	power	nature

Write very fast here!
Fill in the chart on the next page with **single words** that come to you about the theme either of your event memoir or your

personal memoir. This may change again, but it is a way for you to see what words come to you to describe something you would call the theme of your life (or event).

GREAT JOB!

5 M‍inute W‍riting P‍rompt

Take three of the words above—either from the chart I provided, or ones you put in your own chart, and write very fast, incorporating those three words in your writing. See where it goes!

* * * * *

WHAT IS THE THEME OF YOUR EVENT OR PERSONAL MEMOIR at this moment in time? Write a phrase or sentence here:

....

....

....

Step 5: Theme / Secrets

WHY IS A THEME EVEN IMPORTANT?

A theme is important because it is the backbone of your memoir. Think of it this way: as human beings with physical bodies, our theme is to survive and remain alive. In workshops I have given in many places, I ask the attendees to shout out a word that describes their life. Survivor, loneliness, tradition, military, conscientious objector, religion, go-getter, solutions, injustice, money, guilt, success, loss and more are shouted out.

Of course, we have emotional and other needs and wants as well: love, companionship, a job, being heard, having some sense of power and control, wanting to travel, owning a car, overcoming addiction, criminal activity, serving our country in one way or another, raising good crops, helping others, etc.

The people we include in our memoir have wants and needs as well. Sometimes these are at odds with our own wants and needs. This can cause conflict. How did you deal with people who agreed with you or did not agree with you? Did you have to overcome obstacles?

As time goes on, you will see friends who overcame addiction, others who survived verbal and physical abuse, others with self-doubt, anxiety, or lack of confidence. There will be others who discouraged you, slammed you for wanting something different, thwarted you in all kinds of ways. Yet, you persisted, didn't you? Or were you stopped?

Sometimes you gave up, things went south, and you threw up your hands or left a bad situation, not knowing what was going to happen. Maybe you fled to another city or another country to escape a bad relationship, a job you hated, discrimination, war, or crime.

There are infinite ways to react to situations. Your job in your memoir is to figure out what you (the narrator/storyteller) have as your theme. Your theme may not reveal itself to you right away. It might not become evident until you reach the end of your memoir.

When you reread your work, you will see a theme: perseverance, problem-solving, achieving an education, finding a job to support yourself and/or your family. It will become evident as you write your work what the theme of your life is and was. Writing a memoir is about how you have changed throughout your life and a theme helps you to put your life into perspective.

SECRETS

Do you write about family or personal secrets or not? My best advice is in first-draft writing to write everything down. Put anything that comes into your head into your manuscript.

Include secrets you want to reflect on, lies people told you, conflict you endured with family, friends, neighbors—even strangers. These are the juicy tidbits told by you about the nitty-gritty of your life.

Readers love to know what you have gone through and, although I am not a lawyer, and this is only my opinion, as long

Step 5: Theme / Secrets

as you tell the story, but don't call someone else names as in "that *@#%^ so and so," you should be ok. Your memoir is not a revenge story, but may include some very hard times, as well as joyful ones.

If you want to write your memoir for friends and family, legal liability will not be an issue when you describe real events that occurred. However, it may become a problem when your work is published. In publishing contracts, there is often language in which authors promise not to invade privacy, defame character, or otherwise potentially harm others with their words. If the author violates such clauses, there may be significant consequences.

Maybe you told others secrets about abuse, or shared other occurrences and these friends and family were supportive, or maybe they weren't. You have the power to include—or not include—these secrets in your memoir.

Your memoir is a story about your life from your point of view, and as I said earlier in this book, if others say "that is not how I see it," they can write their own memoirs from their own points of view.

In sharing secrets, decide for yourself what you want to divulge. If it is something readers might learn from, as in, "I didn't know anyone but I went through that..." it will be beneficial to someone somewhere wondering if he or she is the only person this particular thing has happened to.

Be prepared for three responses: family and friends saying nothing; a few family and friends denying that what you have

Memoir Writing in 6 Easy Steps

written about actually happened or is true; or readers thanking you and comforting you with their stories.

Use the chart below to help you reveal your secret or a lie you were told.

REVEALING SECRETS OR LIES

Secret or lie to reveal	Who's involved in the secret or lie?	When/Where/How did it happen?
1.		
2.		

STEP 6:
BEGINNING & ENDING

BEGINNINGS

In the writing world, we talk about something called *in media res* —or in the middle of the action. Begin your memoir with a scene —not a chronology—as in "I was born on..."

Why is this important? You are asking your readers to take time out of their busy schedules to be your new best friend. In everyday conversations, we plunge right into our stories: "You'll never guess who I saw today..." "I can't believe this happened..."

If we're speaking to a close friend, we might text or call, saying "I might have to move..." "I just got fired..." "Mom's in hospital..." "I have to sell my house..." "I have decided to leave the country..." "We decided to...divorce...have a baby...move... join the Army...get help...try a new job...try in vitro...or..."

It is with that urgency and inclusion of emotion into our writing at the beginning of our memoir that beckons our readers to stay for a while and read about our lives or events we went through.

An example from Terrence Real's book, *I Don't Want to Talk About It: Overcoming the Secret Legacy of Male Depression*:

Memoir Writing in 6 Easy Steps

> "It took me twenty years to get my father to talk about his own life. I remember the first day he did. I recall the prickly feel of our old yellow couch as we sat together. I was painfully aware of my father's great bulk beside me."

Another example of first page writing. In the Pulitzer-prize winning memoir, *Angela's Ashes,* by Frank McCourt, we read on the first page

> "When I look back on my childhood I wonder how I managed to survive at all. It was, of course, a miserable childhood: the happy childhood is hardly worth your while. Worse than the ordinary miserable childhood is the miserable Irish childhood, and worse yet is the miserable Irish Catholic childhood."

Do you want to know more? To achieve that kind of interest, here is a suggestion:

Take a scene you have written from the middle of your manuscript, put it in at the beginning, and see what happens. Watch the energy of your writing rise as if you were urgently talking to someone and telling them a story that just could not wait to be told. That is good writing and your new best friends—your readers—will turn the pages of your book to see what comes next.

Is it a premonition given to the reader about one's journey through life? Does Frank McCourt's intense description of a "miserable childhood" invite us to explore the difficult issues he will have to deal with as he endures, reflects, and shares with us the difficulties of his life?

Step 6: Beginning & Ending

We don't know. Yet, the writing invites us to join him, and his writing includes both the immediacy of reporting (I am...this is...) and reflections, actual events, how he grew up in poverty, his family, about his life that chewed him up but that he digests in this sensitive memoir.

When you begin the first chapter of your memoir, the reader's introduction to you, include an emotional context. Facts become dry as dust if you do not share your own reactions to events, as well as those of others.

Your detached thoughts are not enough. You must include sensory detail—How did you feel? Did the situation make your skin crawl? Did your face burn or glow? Did your heart beat faster—or seem like it stopped? Were you hungry for love, power, money, success?

It is in the sharing of your emotional state through the scenes you describe as the narrator of your memoir that you captivate your reader. You can do this through dialogue, through showing your reader scenes from your life throughout your memoir.

"My skin was cold on this August day" allows your reader to wonder why. "I was cold. It was August" is another way of writing the same thing. You will find your own style of writing as you go along.

In teaching writing, I always emphasize short paragraphs and not using run-on sentences. You know, the ones that look something like this: *and this and this happened and then this and this didn't happen and we went to and then I saw....* By the end

Memoir Writing in 6 Easy Steps

of all of that, the reader is confused. Remember, you know your story well. Shorter sentences engage the reader faster.

Write as if you were telling your story to a good friend. It is in this abbreviated, everyday way of sharing information, that allows the tone of our voice to convey how we are feeling.

In memoir writing, we share:
- our doubts, fears, conflicts, frustrations,
- possible abuse (physical, emotional or substance),
- successes (no matter how small), failures,
- decisions (good or bad),
- wrestling with hard times,
- surviving job losses,
- living in a house for the first time,
- getting into a college you wanted to go to (or not),
- figuring out your own identity apart from your family,
- parenting (or not), being taken seriously (or not),
- moving from a place we love into an uncertain place,
- financial hard times (and good times),
- illness (your own or a family member's),
- death of a family member and feeling alone,
- travel (the good and the bad)
- and much more.

Step 6: Beginning & Ending

Sue Massey's memoir, *Letter from the Heart. The Real Story Behind the Iconic Photograph* is about the struggle to save their family farm. A Farm Aid concert was held on their behalf, but that didn't help the inevitable. Her first sentences in Chapter 1, Blowin' in the Wind, are:

> "I opened my eyes as if it were any other morning. Glancing at my husband Kenny's scrunched pillow, then at our alarm clock, I saw it was six thirty. In just one hour, we would learn the fate of our small business—the family-owned business we had poured our heart and soul into for over two decades."

As we get older—say, past forty—we begin to reflect on our lives. We have lived through the daily permutations of life. No matter what economic, cultural, racial, or ethnic background— *YOUR LIFE MATTERS*. The events that happen to you are worthy of noting in a memoir. Your book-length memoir about your life is important to others.

Why? you ask. We are all travelers on this planet and share universal emotions and have survived things we never thought we would have to endure. I teach people of all ages, economic conditions, ethnicities, and racial makeup—and this holds true for the stories people have shared with me over the years.

In a poor community, survival can mean a single mom living in a trailer in the country. The trailer burns down on Christmas Eve (a true story), and she puts her kids outside and runs inside to get her child's shoes because it is so cold. A resale shop near this trailer finds out and immediately gathers clothing for the family, others find them somewhere to live, others bring presents for the kids.

It can mean being in an upscale community and an owner of a small business built over years of hard daily work discovers his accountant has been stealing from him. To settle some of his affairs, he has to short-sale his house and use his retirement money to cover his losses.

It might be a retired dentist moving from an urban to a rural community in a different state and writing about someone in a previous practice causing serious damage to unsuspecting patients and how she took a leap and reported this person to the licensing board.

Maybe it is about a young white family renting an apartment, then buying a house and subletting their apartment to a black family. This was back in the days before anti-discrimination laws were passed—when realtors were steering people away from certain communities.

Or a tennis player making it into the world circuit even though he was born poor with no funds to pay for tennis coaches or even how to gain financial backing. This happened through sheer determination and hard work. Sleeping in his car or on a beach, with no funds for food, but driven by a passion for tennis and a force within him to be the best.

* * * * *

Step 6: Beginning & Ending

The world needs your memoir—because it gives others hope. They might say "wow, the author survived that...." and know that somehow they can survive the things happening in their life, too.

Begin your memoir in the middle of a scene, in the middle of a dialogue or action, and then go on to the other various chapters and scenes in your memoir.

Again, remember, you have now invited new friends to spend time with you—smile and enjoy the satisfaction of extending the invitation.

THE LAST CHAPTER

You brave person. You worked hard to get here. This is NOT the end of your story, which is comprised of your reflections about your life story or the event you have written about.

TIP: Try writing this chapter first. Yes, you read that right. Tackle this chapter first, because it allows you to begin where you are in your life right now. You are writing this chapter, wherever you find yourself in age, class, race, or ethnicity. Right now.

Writing this last chapter first allows you—in the present tense—as in "I think..." "I know ..." "I wonder ..." "I am still angry ..." "I forgive ..." "I survived ..."—to reflect on the event or book-length memoir you are either about to write, or have written.

You can write about what you learned, what worked, what didn't work, what you wish you had tried, what you would like readers and/or family to learn about you. You can be philosophical or wonder if life is about free will and/or is determined by something else.

You can ponder what would have happened had your job/marriage not ended or wonder if moving to another location helped or hindered you.

Maybe you laugh at your mistakes. Dire things that took over your mind and heart at various times in your life might not seem, in hindsight, so terrible. Or maybe they were disasters that led you to find other skills, or meet other people, or learn more about your financial or emotional life. Or maybe they didn't. Write about these things.

Did you reconcile with people in your life? Did you gain understanding of them—did you miss them when they died? Did you want to say something to them even though friends, family, or colleagues are no longer with you? Then say it here, in this last chapter, in your own words. "I always want to tell you this …" "I hated it when you did this …" "I still love you …" Or…

Do you have regrets? Did you overcome self-doubt? Does it do any good to punish yourself over and over for things you did not do? Did people you trusted betray you—and how do you feel about that now?

Pulitzer Prize-winning poet Robert Penn Warren said:

> "…for the self is never to be found, but must be created, not the happy accident of passivity, but the product of a thousand actions, large and small,

Step 6: Beginning & Ending

conscious or unconscious, performed not 'away from it all' but in the face of 'it all,' for better or for worse, in work and leisure rather than in free time."

This is not the end of your life, only the end of the part of your life you have lived up until now.

WRITING EXERCISE No. 1.
Write for 10 minutes about what you would like to say to yourself at age 16 or 18. Is there advice you would like your younger self to know? Write very fast and see where it goes.

WRITING EXERCISE No. 2.
Write for 10 minutes about what you would like to say to your children, grandchildren, or future generations. What advice would you give them?

WRITING EXERCISE No. 3.
Write for 10 minutes about what you have learned during your life or how you might have handled a life-changing event you wrote about differently.

WRITING EXERCISE No. 4.
Write for 10 minutes about the theme of your life. Return to your list of scenes and look again at the themes of your life. Has it changed?

Memoir Writing in 6 Easy Steps

Notes

WRAPPING IT UP

Writing a memoir about your life is living proof that you were here on this planet. It is not a grave marker or a tombstone standing in a grassy place somewhere. Or an urn on a shelf—or someone else's shelf—filled with who you used to be.

Your memoir is a document you write to help others as they navigate their own lives. "*What?*" you ask. If you choose to publish your memoir, it might help others. *My memoir could help others?* Yes, it might. Someone sitting in a small town somewhere in the middle of nowhere might read your work and be comforted by how you faced the dilemmas in your life. Even if the dilemmas didn't necessarily have happy endings. You survived.

If your memoir is intended for friends and family, you have given them the best gift you could ever give them: a narrative , told in your own voice, about your life. They will be surprised to learn about what you did, what worked out for you, what did not work out.

A long time ago, my husband's uncle published a book about my husband's family genealogy. It is an extensive look back at his family's history. Our children each have a copy of it, as do we.

Memoir Writing in 6 Easy Steps

We cherish the thoughts of those who went before my husband was born.

In this book, you have learned about the writing elements that comprise a memoir:

- What the theme of your life might be
- How to handle that negative freeloader living in your brain, spouting comments like, "You can't write a memoir." (I think those freeloaders come with our DNA). It is powerful when you say to the freeloader, "I've got this. Don't worry."
- Remember my mantra: "There is no such thing as perfection; there is only good enough. We can strive to make something good, but perfection is a myth that keeps us from achieving our goals."

To recap the 6 steps to writing your memoir:

- **Step 1: CHARACTERS AND NARRATOR.** You learned about yourself as the narrator (hero). You learned how to define and write about major and minor characters who will appear in your memoir.
- **Step 2: SCENES.** You learned how to figure out the scenes you want to include and how to write a scene that includes a beginning, middle, and end.
- **Step 3: CONFLICT AND ANGER.** This is often the hardest thing to write about. We have times when we—or others—are in conflict. Sometimes we—or someone else—gets angry. Sometimes it is righteous anger, sometimes we regret getting angry. Sometimes others apologize; sometimes they don't. Whatever happens, conflict arises. Why is conflict important

in a memoir? Because it completes the narrative arc. In other words, conflict has to be in our lives at some point or another. Your memoir would be dry and boring if it didn't include some sort of conflict.

Readers love being propelled through scenes of conflict and keep flipping pages to see what will happen next. They also learn how you handled the conflict (or didn't) and they feel comforted knowing that someone else got angry and had to resolve (or couldn't) a difficult situation.

- **Step 4: DIALOGUE.** You learned to write down what you do all day long: speak in dialogue to another human being. (Well, OK, we sometimes talk to our pets, too.) You learned the importance of including dialogue in your memoir. This bears repeating:
    - *Direct dialogue*—a conversation you remember word for word and place in quotation marks.
    - *Indirect dialogue*—a summary of a dialogue that appears in the storytelling narrative. It happens when the reader needs to know the conversation took place, but doesn't need to know the actual words spoken. There are no quotation marks around this dialogue.
    - *Paraphrased dialogue*—in which we remember the gist of a conversation, but not word for word. There are no quotation marks around this dialogue.
- **Step 5: THEME AND SECRETS.** What is the theme of your life? Do you write about secrets you have?
- **Step 6: BEGINNINGS AND ENDINGS.**
    - BEGINNINGS. Begin your memoir in the middle of a scene. Maybe a scene from the middle of your

Memoir Writing in 6 Easy Steps

memoir, a scene that invites your reader to want to learn more.

- ENDINGS. Now you can look at the theme of your life that you wrote down at the beginning of the book. Did it change as you wrote your memoir? What did you learn during your lifetime? How did you grow in understanding the world, your life, the lives of others? What have you learned that you would want others to know about?

I AM SO PROUD OF YOU FOR WORKING ON THIS MEMOIR OF YOUR LIFE AND I CAN HARDLY WAIT TO READ IT!

—Sue Roupp

REFERENCES

Allende, Isabelle. *Paula.* Harper Collins Publishers, 1994.

Karr, Mary. *Lit.* Harper Collins, 2009.

King, Stephen. *On Writing: A Memoir of the Craft.* Charles Scribner's Sons, 2000, republished in 2010.

Lewis, Sinclair. *Arrowsmith.* Harcourt Brace Publisher, 1925.

Massey, Sue. *Letter from the Heart: the Real Story Behind the Iconic Photograph.* Little Creek Press. A Division of Kristin Mitchell Design, LLC, 2014.

McCourt, Frank. *Angela's Ashes.* Scribner, 1996.

Real, Terrence. *I Don't Want to Talk About It: Overcoming the Secret Legacy of Male Depression.* Scribner, 1997.

Wadeson, Harriet Claire. LCSW, ATR-BC, HLM, *Journaling Cancer in Words and Images: Caught in the Clutch of the Crab.* Charles C. Thomas Publisher, Ltd., 2011.

Warren, Robert Penn, *Jefferson Lecture in the Humanities.* Harvard University Press, 1974.

ACKNOWLEDGMENTS

To my husband, who has always been by my side gently encouraging me in all my endeavors. To our children and their partners and families, who have always been my inspiration as they move through their endearing and successful lives.

To my colleagues and friends, Christine DeSmet and Laurie Scheer, at UW-Madison, who gave me a chance years ago to teach at the UW Writers' Institute.

To those I have taught—and learned so much from—over the many years I have taught memoir, creative writing, and poetry.

To so many friends on the north shore of Chicago among them: Judith Kaufman (East on Central), Jennifer Dotson (highlandpark-poetry.com).

Last and not least, to my mom and dad, who were baffled about how I could support myself with a college degree. For whom the word "career" did not exist. I have never forgotten where I came

Memoir Writing in 6 Easy Steps

from, the hard work, honesty, and helping others values you taught me.

This book continues those values, helping others value their lives by remembering THEIR LIVES COUNT, TOO.

ABOUT THE AUTHOR

Sue Roupp has been teaching memoir writing, fiction, non-fiction, and poetry for 20 years. Classes include: Chris Vogler, author of the *Hero's Journey*; Billy Collins/poetry, Piven Theater Workshop; certified national public speaker. Off-Campus Writers Workshop, Winnetka, IL. (200 writers), Guest editor of *East on Central*, poetry judge: highlandparkpoetry.com; State Board League of VT Writers; columns: Independent Bookstores Nationwide, TV show: smalltalk etc., workshops: UW Madison Writers Institute; Ragdale, Women's Exchange; ArtStart/Rhinelander, WI; Marywood Spiritual Center. Sue offers ongoing private classes/workshops/speeches.

Please visit her at www.sueroupp.com

www.ingramcontent.com/pod-product-compliance
Lightning Source LLC
Chambersburg PA
CBHW051659090426
42736CB00013B/2445